Utaziah

Life - A Creation Of Time
A Modern Day Translation of Universal Truth

Channelled By

Rev A Farley

Spiritual Messenger/Leader for the Utaziah Faith

http://www.utaziah.com

authorHOUSE®

AuthorHouse™ UK Ltd.
500 Avebury Boulevard
Central Milton Keynes, MK9 2BE
www.authorhouse.co.uk
Phone: 08001974150

First published by AuthorHouse 2/8/2008

ISBN: 978-1-4343-5329-0 (sc)

Printed in the United States of America
Bloomington, Indiana

This book is printed on acid-free paper.

Contents

For One Person to stand alone in what they Believe
Takes Strength received from their Source

For Two People to stand together in what they Believe
Takes Respect and Understanding

For Three People to stand together in what they Believe
Takes Courage and Wisdom

... and for You All to Believe takes Time

Introduction

The Utaziah Faith to me is a way of life, a constant changing cycle within myself and each one of you, forever striving to improve and create new ways of thinking and learning to enjoy the fruits that life has to offer. No matter how simplistic they may seem but bringing joy and wonder at what you have experienced either by what you have done yourself or the ever changing beauty of nature and the seasons.

I have found the Truth according to my perception but continued to search for further knowledge to enhance and stimulate my being on an Emotional, Physical, Mental and Spiritual Level because what I believe in is all I have to understand and learn. Only time will tell where my future lies and like all of you, our destiny's are but a drop of water in an endless well of existence and time. Time and time again you re-birth to right the wrongs of the past in order to make the future your home.

To all who read this book, all I ask is that you read it with an open mind and a clear consciousness. All I ask is that you learn for yourselves right from wrong, for your beliefs are what guides you and influences you in all you do. Belief in yourself is paramount for your own survival but if you can learn to believe in others then the peace you will feel is one of love.

Humanity is just one race living together on a beautiful planet that's floating through space. The differences you share as a race are what make you unique and fruitful in the knowledge of life. It really doesn't matter what colour, race, creed, sexuality, orientation or faith you are or what you call it, as there can be only One God or Goddess.

Albeit not all interpretations are the same and they do differ in many ways, but the general message is the same and that is to love and help your fellow beings in times of trouble and to rejoice and triumph when you have had success in your life or by bringing joy to others.

You see each individual Life Force Energy needs different things to fuel it:

> The Body needs Food, Drink and Sex

> The Mind needs Stimulation, Information and Guidance

> The Emotions need Control, Discipline and Love

> The Soul needs Freedom and Peace

The Whole Entity needs to be Understood and Respected for its achievements on a Spiritual, Physical, Emotional and Mental Level of Existence creating a Balance both Internally and Externally.

These needs belong to every living person, as you all need them in various forms to survive, so it doesn't matter what colour or culture you were raised in, as everybody has these basic needs in common. So the differences are what you yourselves create and pass down to your children from generation to generation.

You install in them what you believe and that includes all of your shortcomings and prejudices which you learnt from what was passed down to you by Society, Your Peers, Your Parents and Families telling you How it is and How it should be.

So they don't teach or guide you with an open mind but install their views and opinions upon future generations, so in turn creating the problems you have today Racially, Sexually, Religiously and Socially.

If you do not start to learn about each other and respect the differences you share, then your children will either become the beneficiaries of a Paradise or the Victims of the Seeds You have Sown.

For the Children are the Future but unless they are guided to reject prejudice in all its forms and embrace the wonders of a world open with Opportunity and Unity then an uncertain future for Humanity will continue to reign.

Just like Humanity which at present is a delicate egg shell waiting to give birth to a new age of being on all levels, things will only get worse and like a disease can ravish the body, then the disease called Prejudicial Hatred and Blind Fear through lack of Understanding will no doubt engulf your world until those who seek to walk with blinkers have destroyed the very place that gives you Life and Sanctuary.

This is all because they didn't choose to think for themselves or make choices based on the Whole Truth through knowledge and learning and not the ones they were told as children. The beauty of being an adult human being is that you have the right and ability to cast down the chains which were placed upon you as a child and embrace a new way of thinking based on the Truth. By embracing the Real World in which you live which is full of different colours, smells and pleasures.

Just think how bland it would be if you had to eat the same meal every time you ate, No Variety, just the same old things. Well walking with Blind Faith is actually the same because how do you know whether or not the food on the next table is tasty unless you have tried it.

So, Break Free from the restrictions that you place upon yourselves and those that are placed upon you by other people who cannot understand your needs and desires as they aren't living in your body and experiencing your life.
All they are doing is sharing the same time and space and that's only if you want them too, as life is One Big Choice and it all starts with You.

If Freedom is the right of everyone, then why do you suppress the right to be Free?

Freedom is achieved within yourself, guidance to achieve this is provided for you in various forms and faiths. The best method is to check out and read what you are drawn to and then take the bits that you need to enable you to further your own Spiritual, Physical, Emotional and Mental Journey of Growth and Understanding.

Exploring and Experiencing different faiths and beliefs is the secret to achieving Inner Freedom thus enabling Outer Freedom through this process. God/Goddess provides you with the basic Teachings and Guidance to achieving a good life but He/She gave you all Free Will to choose how you live it.

For if a man has eyes to see, it doesn't mean to say he actually sees, for a Blind Man's sight might be more realistic and perceptive, So Who Sees More?

Love is the Uniting Force that can conquer Life's Obstacles; Love of yourself is very important but after that Love for your fellow beings will help elevate Humanity to another level:

Inner Love Creates Outer Love
Inner Peace Creates Outer Peace
A Genuine concurrent flow of what has gone before

WORLD PEACE is very possible, if you all decide to create it, as the Vision is the Idea, the Action is to implement what you have started to learn, so you can enhance yourself primarily and create your own balance. Once this is completed you can start to help and enhance other people's lives, this being a knock on effect and irreversible.

Once you have chosen this path then your perception will be altered from what you used to perceive, Your World will look different through the same eyes but a widened consciousness.

The Future is never Guaranteed, it is the Actions of Today that determine Our Tomorrow. For what is the Reason when the Cause is yet to be established, for the Reason enhances the Action and the Action creates the Cause.

No one view is correct for each person has to judge for themselves what is right for their existence. I hope you Believe and find your path to Enlightenment and Peace through this channelled information that has been written and expressed.

I shall endeavour to seek out the Knowledge to enhance my life and other people's lives according to my perception and need, you too can only do the same for your lives for each one of you is different and your perceptions of the Truth may vary.

Hopefully in time all of Humanity as a race will take a Deep Breath and realize it is good to be alive and start enjoying Your World instead of Destroying it and Each Other.

So Make Your Choices Carefully, for they will truly depict -

Your Fate

I hope you enjoy the book XXXX
ADF

1
GENETIC

The Journey

The Mirror of Life
Is only a vision of time
Your Mirror of Life
Is just a Maze called your Mind
For life is a journey
Unforeseen, Unforetold
So travel down it lightly my friend
And embrace your Pure Soul

Genetic

Life's journey is a never ending cycle of Birth, Life, Death, Re-Birth, and the wheel continues turning. It starts with your physical conception creating a fusion of Genetic Energy. The only thing your parents gave you, which you cannot change, is your genetic make-up.

What they cannot give you is your Individualistic Soul which is who you are now and have always been and will be again in the future depending on what you have learnt and acquired in this lifetime.

They cannot even tell you about it or what it needs or desires to make it happy and fulfilled only you can know this by learning and gathering knowledge on what interests you Emotionally, Physically, Mentally and Spiritually only you can make those choices.

People say 'That you only have one life so live it', well this is true whilst you are walking about on this earth, but when you die you are reborn again into another body, as Human Beings are primarily energy and your Soul is where all your knowledge and energy from past lives is stored. By listening to your heart and conscience you can be guided by the knowledge you had gathered previously.

How many times have you experienced being able to do something without being trained or you know certain facts and knowledge on a subject yet you have never read the book! Well the chances are that you acquired the ability or knowledge in a previous life and like a computer file you have recalled the program which was downloaded into your Soul.

So let me take you to a place where life is just sections, different levels, within which you all shall travel, maybe not now but in the future depending upon your behaviour in this particular life cycle.

The place is unknown, your destination is now, the time is immaterial but with your dreams you can all travel to a place called Utaziah.

Utaziah

Where is it? Everybody asks!
They all want to know
A place of Fulfilment, Love, Hope and a Future
As you sit listening to various music
You think as you look at the sky
The sun is setting, the air is thin
So that is where my Utaziah begins
A Utopia of Perfection and Dreams
All rolled into one
You All are welcome there

To live the Utazian Lifestyle, you do not need to sacrifice the things in life that you enjoy or what gives you pleasure. To stop enjoying these things is to deprive yourself of something that stimulates your emotions and to suppress the emotions is to destroy part of who you are and what's the point of that!

It won't make you happy and so you start to ride the downward spiral of disillusionment and depression (for which society believes medication and pills are the answers) by denying yourself the very things that will enhance your life.

As long as these things do not infringe upon another person's right of choice or impose your will upon another person, for this is wrong just because you get a kick out of it. This is not only unfair but you do not have the right to try to control or subject another being, be it a Human or an Animal to suffering in order to make you feel good.

An Unknown Entity

The campfire glistens in the faded daylight
The Air is thin with smoke, icy smoke
The music flickers through your ears
Taking in every little sound
Interpreting it to be your entire existence
The flames grow then die
Its embers glowing with the secrets of life
By adding fuel to the fire
You can all create a new energy
An Unknown Entity, A Mysterious Charm
Search within its flames
For you'll see all and be one!

YOU are the Unknown Entity; from the day you were born you have soaked up information by:

> What you hear, what you see
> What you taste, what you smell
> What you touch and What you are told!!!

The fuel needed to enable you to grow and become strong within yourself is:

> Food and Drink to energise and regenerate the body

> Access to all Knowledge to enable you to expand your mind, so you can make informed choices and decisions

> Freedom to express yourself without suppression, whatever forms it may come in and from wherever it may come from

As you grow stronger your energy will flow better because you will have started to lift the restrictions placed upon you by freeing your mind, therefore embracing your mysterious charm which is the Real You created by You and no one else.

By searching within yourself to discover your own True Flame, True Light, True Love and the Liberty and Freedom to express it, then you will experience Your First Love which is Yourself, so see all and become one with Yourself.

To You All I Say

Believe in Your Dreams
Believe in Yourself
Do you now know why?
The Soul replaces the Man
Do you now understand?

Life is Eternal but only You
Can Chart Its Course
By Your Actions and Your Thoughts
For it is by these means you travel
You already have Eternal Life
But it is up to you how you live it

For Your Soul is You now
And forever shall be
You never die, You just take on
Another Transformation
Forever Growing and Learning

It is Your Thoughts and Dreams
Which can change what is
To what will be

You are the Masters of your Own Destiny
And Your Body
Your chariot forever running
In one form or another
One cannot survive without the other
But they can lie dormant
Until their time to rise
Is to begin again

If a person is to be free
They firstly have to meet their Soul
For here is their Life Force
Here is their Core
No greater fear doth anyone know
Than the conclusion to years gone by

Freedom of Choice
Is to have
Freedom of the Spirit
For this you need
Freedom of the Mind
For it is only by the LAW
That Learning All Wisdom
Is the only True Path to Enlightenment

SO

Face your Fears
And Believe You are Strong
Embrace the Truth
Your Light from within
Believe in the Truth
And Hear Your Soul Sing

Free Your Mind
To Free Your Spirit
Free Your Soul
Encased in its shell
You are the Masters of what will be
You are the ones
You must live the Dream

A Penny

A Penny for a thought
That Single Wish, That Single Song
A Small Price to pay
To find a Single Creation

So if Reality is an Illusion
Created by Your Own Imaginations
Then Perhaps
You are All just a Vision
For Dreams are just Reality in the Making
So Live The Dream

2
RE-BIRTHING PROCESS

Re-Birthing Process

The world you perceive to be around you, will not be your world, just another dimension/extension of your own reality.

If you open the door to a new life beyond your present reality, then your perception of what is real will be enhanced by the process which you have undertaken. Therefore before you enter this new life, you have to follow a process of Self Understanding in order to enable you to accept the realm within which you shall enter.

Once you have found your True Identity and Understanding, only then will the acceptance of a new life endeavour you to enhance your mind and therefore you will be able to create an environment for yourself, which will enable all forms of life to interact in harmony and as one.

To acquire the knowledge to enable you to acquire the key to your universe, you have to first of all follow the process described below:

1)   **Find out Who and What You Are**

In order to do this, you will need to look at all the good and bad aspects of your personality, which you all have. You will need to discover what makes you happy, what you enjoy, what you find fulfilling and satisfying, what stimulates you Mentally, Emotionally, Physically, and Spiritually basically you need to reintroduce yourself to yourself.

The Key here is to experiment with all aspects of your life, worrying about what society judges as to what is right or wrong isn't what is important. As long as what you are doing is not illegal and you are not hurting anyone else during the process then who is to judge or decide whether or not you have to do or practice or live your life a certain way.

Only by trying new things will you find out whether or not they are right for you, so take the step and break the mould (whatever that may be). Discover for yourself new ways of looking at things and new experiences for you to embrace, in order for you to fulfil your truly enlightened perception.

As the word Enlightenment states after this process of Self Understanding you will feel Lightened from all those burdens that have been put upon you and from which you are now free to be yourself.

2)   Understand Why You Are Here and For What Purpose

You are here on this earth to have an experience Physically, Mentally, Emotionally and Spiritually. In order to enable you to experience this fully, you need to let go of your inhibitions and open your mind to new ways of living and experiencing your life.

The problem most of you have is that you continually try to seek the approval of other people within society whilst forgetting that you too have a voice and you too need to discover the aspects of life that bring you joy. By seeking the approval of others in the way you live your life, you aren't living for yourself but for them and by their Standards and Morals which may not be perfect anyway.

This will eventually lead to you repressing your emotions and to an unhappy and unfulfilling life. Now is this what you really want? I very much doubt it, so start living for you and experience the wonders that life has to offer YOU !!

The purpose of your life is to have fun and enjoy being alive by doing what makes you happy and by this I mean:

Doing a job you enjoy
Living a lifestyle you like
Following a Faith you can Believe in and what doesn't tell you what to do but offers real guidance and opportunity for you to grow into an individual. Don't become a sheep or someone's puppet with them pulling the strings and you just dancing to their tune because everybody else is doing so.

So don't be the Puppet, be the Puppet Master and pull your own string.

Be an Individual and look at other Faiths, you never know you may find what you have been looking for and if not then you may find something which can enhance what you already practice. Remember Variety is the Spice of Life, So Diversify.

3) **Perception of the Inner Self and Dual Personality/Side to your character**

Perception of your Inner Self is being aware that it exists and it has needs and desires, which can only be fulfilled by having an experience.

The dual personality/side to you is the good and bad side of your nature. You need to understand both of theses so it's a case of being cruel to be kind and you must look at yourself objectively. Don't make the mistake of looking at just your good points because it is the bad points that need work on.

4) **Accept your reality for what it is 'An Illusion' and relate the theoretical knowledge you have gathered and cross reference the underlining mechanics of the Universe in order to evaluate the function of Time, Matter and Energy.**

The reason your reality is an illusion is because the people who run your world keep secrets from the masses and the leaders of your world keep the people in an illusionary state, which is their projection of a reality they feel is good enough for you.

The Governing bodies of your world are out for their own gain and create rules and restrictions so that the people aren't really free, they are made to think they are but in Reality you are slaves to their cause and not your own.

Although you need rules within a society in order to avoid chaos and anarchy, like all things in life, there are good ones and bad ones and any action that stops an individual from fulfilling their true potential is a crime against Humanity.

The Religious Leaders of your world are happy to sit in their ivory towers and watch the people suffer whilst they feed off the bones and bodies of the dying. Now, I don't just mean a physical death but a Spiritual one where they are no longer interested in freeing your Soul but caging it in a prison and asking to be paid for the privilege and the pleasure.

These so-called Religious Organisations have a physical wealth which could quite easily right the wrongs inflicted upon Humanity by War, Famine and Greed but they won't give up their wealth because they are afraid they will lose their power along with it.

If their Faith was so strong and just then why fear poverty in the name of a good cause? The reason for this is because they fear more will be spent out then what will be coming in, as they always like their purses and begging bowls to be full. So it's a shame the same full bounty can't be shared by the suffering and starving in your world, this is Pure Greed and Pride on their behalf as they fear losing their Power, Control and Status within Society.

Blind Faith... the Miracle is giving you the foresight to be able to see the Truth by removing the veil of Illusion from your eyes and open your minds to the True Reality and Potential within yourselves and not to fill their pockets as these religions will have you believe, for the Kingdom of Heaven, Nirvana, or whatever you may call the resting place for the soul, cannot be bought into ... so you cannot buy your way to salvation because it is what is in your heart and by your actions that will determine the next level of existence next time around, not how much you have paid for sanctuary when your time comes to leave this lifetime for the next.

So don't dig deep into your purses in order to gain favour from on high, dig Deep into your Soul as the wealth of Knowledge you will find there is for you to enjoy your life with. This was the Miracle/Gift each and every one of you was meant to receive. True Enlightenment through God/Goddesses True Teachings, Guidance and LAW.

As was spoken "Let There Be Light",

The light that was spoken of was Enlightenment for All Humanity to grow and blossom with the Knowledge through God/Goddesses Teachings, Guidance and LAW and not for the chosen few who hide the truth of the real teachings.

In the beginning He sent His First Archangel Lucifer (Which means Light Bringer or Bringer of Enlightenment) who sat by His Right

13

Hand Side, His Anointed One. Being the Alpha and the Omega, the beginning and the end, She came to bring His Teachings, Guidance and LAW to All Humanity at your beginning so that you could live your lives in Peace, Harmony and Prosperously through the hard work and efforts you had made.

So at the end of the Old Era and the Beginning of the New Era, A Golden Age for Humanity shall be born (The concurrent flow of what has gone before and has returned again) the cycle has come full circle to begin again once more.

So once again He says "Let There Be Enlightenment" for All Humanity through His Teachings, Guidance and LAW incorporating All Faiths of your world, as they all offer something for each and every one of you to benefit from and enhance your well being. For example Meditation, Incense Rituals, Yoga, Prayer, Chanting, Music and many more wonderful practices to help stimulate your Mind, Body and Soul to grow and relax and be stimulated by the experiences you have had.

This is why the term 'Selling Your Soul' was invented, so that when the day came for you to be free, you still retained your most precious asset and identity which is You as a Whole, Mentally, Physically, Emotionally and Spiritually.

So this is the underlining mechanics of Your Universe (Earth) and the function is for those in Power across the board to become Healthy, Wealth and Free to spread the lies. Now the real function should be for the masses to be able to live and enjoy their lives, without being treated like Mushrooms (Fed on shit and kept in the dark) under the United Umbrella of Freedom and Faith.

Humanity deserves to be free from a world where Governments and Religious Leaders fight continuous Wars in the name of Peace and God/Goddess, like they have done throughout the ages, when really it's over Land, Oil and World Resources which if Controlled means Power and Control over Humanity for them.

God/Goddess does not tell people to fight Holy Wars; these are the Actions of Spiritually Misguided People who want an excuse to cause chaos rather than to have the courage to build a world where you can live as one. To hide behind your Faith to cause such harm is not Spirituality or Religion as it benefits no-one and only causes Pain and Suffering.

This would indeed be a mirror image of what is inside these people as the inner reflects the outer and from where I am standing they need to reassess their faith as it obviously isn't making them happy.

5) **Once you have followed the above process – think again – about what it is you really need. For if the Hunger outweighs the Craving then knowledge and Wisdom will unlock the doors to an understanding of the Cosmic Dance, so you can enhance your mind. Once you have perceived your True Need, then the Desire becomes Reality and the Reality is the inevitable integration of Life, The Universe and The Source.**

The above process is inevitable, there are no short cuts. Unless you are able to perceive Who and What you are, then and only then will you be able to start the Re-Birthing Process.
The answers are there, but unless you embrace the Truth about yourself with open arms and foresight, the journey will be long and it will be hard. Only you know what it is you want from life, so don't be afraid to go after what you need to make your life better even if society disagrees with your choices. As long as you are not hurting another being in the process or doing something, which is considered illegal. By that I mean abusing or stealing from another person to achieve your aims. Then you should feel free to chase your dreams and desires without prejudice or judgement from those who are small minded and discriminative.

Life is a Game within which you are just players; success is just a roll of the dice. In order to climb the stairway you first of all have to understand the fundamental elements contained within life and then re-create the energy by changing yourself and redirecting it by you becoming a part of a more Global Change.

Then you will be completing the Quest and Knowledgeable Challenge.

Then and Only Then can you start to act upon what it is you have learnt and complete your Re-Birth.

Some of you will receive Enlightenment through this process in order to ENHANCE the Growth/Survival of Humanity and your own interaction with other Worlds and Life Forces.

3

GOD / GODDESS LAW

God / Goddess Law

The LAW of GOD/GODDESS is to Learn All Wisdom. In your society today you are told by various Spiritual and Religious Groups that if you practice certain acts, then you will suffer for your actions accordingly.

So let's look at what defines Karma/Sin. Karma/Sin is when you do an action which causes hurt and suffering to another being, be it Human or Animal, which they haven't given consent for you to do.

Just because you may have had or think a bad thought this does not constitute being punished under God/Goddess Law. If that were the case, then how can you debate within yourself the right course of action to take with regards to that particular thought, therefore not allowing you the freedom to make the right choice.

It is the action combined with a bad thought that depicts Bad Karma/Sin, so this is why you are able to think things through. If you continued with your train of thought and commit a bad act to another being, then you Deserve to be Punished, not only by the legal systems within your society but by the Universe as a whole.

No-one has the right to make other beings suffer, no matter what their status is in your society or who they think they are. For in your society if a person holds a powerful position or has wealth or fame then they are revered, but in the Grand Scheme of things they are just a tiny grain of sand in the ocean of Time and Space and are accountable to a Higher Form of Justice beyond their influence of your world and God/Goddess Justice is based upon our actions not your status, wealth or position.

Using the excuse that 'I had a bad childhood and was treated badly" won't wash, as all of you know right from wrong and just because your childhood was bad, it doesn't mean to say your adulthood should be. You now have the choice to make the changes in your life to make it better, anyone could find something or someone to blame for what you have done wrong. No doubt bad things have happened to all of you at some point in your lives, so why put another being through the torment and pain you suffered and didn't like there is **No Excuse**.

Committing an Act of Mental, Physical, Emotional, Verbal or Spiritual Violence and Abuse, will incur you Punishment in whatever form it may take. You may not receive it in this life but you can be sure it will be dealt out in the next.

If you do not believe this to be so and it doesn't matter as your life is good now and you feel you can do what you want to whomever you want, whenever you want then go ahead and continue on your path. I can guarantee that next time round you will be asking yourself this question 'What have I done wrong in order for my life to be so shit". Well maybe in that life you haven't but in the previous one you may well have committed such acts against another which caused them to suffer and so it is your turn to experience the bottom of the wheel whilst they are at the top.

Now don't think because you have trampled and lie your way to the top that it is because you are good, for you would be wrong to think this.

Being successful does not mean you are a good person as it is circumstance and other peoples influence and help which probably went a long way to getting you to where you are now.

If in the process for you to succeed another being suffered at your hands, then think again about redressing the balance before it is too late. As when you are dead and gone, you can't change what has been done or committed; this can only be done whilst you are living that life.

If you have a particular choice of sexual practice then, as long as the parties involved are consenting adults, anything goes. There is **No Punishment** for enjoying these pleasures as some would have you believe. This is not an area where God/Goddess Law has any interest in as it isn't causing harm to anyone.

The only time God/Goddess Law comes into play is when you commit an act without consent which causes pain and suffering knowingly and on purpose. For that you DESERVE TO SUFFER because you should have known better.

These acts are considered under God/Goddess Law to be the most serious and will incur Severe Punishment without Mercy of any kind:

1) **Child Abuse**

2) **Murder**

3) **Rape**

4) **Violence to another being, no matter what form it may take**

5) **To kill or cause suffering in God/Goddesses Name therefore bringing God/Goddesses Love for Humanity into question, causing doubt through Greed, Power and Control of all natural resources from Oil and Land To Food and Water. As what is needed to survive is provided for Humanity on this planet for all to benefit from not just those who can afford it.**

The Guidelines to follow to avoid Punishment are:

1) **Respect**

Be Respectful of other people and their belongings within your community and society, DO NOT take what is not yours.

Be polite and friendly

Have Respect for yourself and others choice of lifestyle and belief

Be Respectful to other beings who inhabit the Earth

Be Respectful to your planet and nature as it sustains your life, for without it you do not exist

2) **Balance**

Try to create a balance in your life on all levels

Try to replenish the balance within nature when the balance has been de-stabilised, replace what you have taken or destroyed, thus in turn ensuring your own survival and the survival for future generations

3)   Understanding

Try to be more understanding about different people, cultures, beliefs and lifestyles. Take a look at new ways of doing things even if they don't turn out to be right for you. By checking them out, it will enable you to have a better and wider understanding, therefore opening your mind to new opportunities and potential.

4)   Love

Learn to love yourself because if you don't love you then how can you expect anybody else to. Give love to those you know, as love comes in many forms:

Helping someone, caring for someone
Listening to someone, taking time to be with someone
Holding someone and allowing someone to do the same for you

By offering a little bit of love, you in turn will be loved

5)   Experience

Experience is gained through taking the time to learn about new things. If you haven't experienced something then you cannot comment on it or give an opinion because you have no knowledge of what you are talking about.

Too many people in your world pass comment on subjects they have no experience in and by making a judgement on other people who may practice different lifestyles to them isn't fair. They are in fact just making an assumption which isn't based on factual knowledge but pure fantasy inside their heads, or on other people's views and opinions.

Before passing comment or judgement on the way another person lives their life a particular way, the best thing to do is experience it and if it isn't right for you then that is your choice but do not deny another person theirs.

Some people believe that experience is gained through getting older, this is for the most part true, but just because a person is of a particular age, it doesn't mean to say that they are always right or know more.

Most of the prejudices, discrimination and lack of true understanding of the Truth is because of what was passed down from previous generations who never really questioned their elders principles or beliefs they just accepted that they were right.

Whereas time has proven that that way of thinking and domination has bought you to the way in which your world is now.

Technologically you have advanced but Spiritually and Personally you are no different to what you were thousands of years ago. All because the people who ruled the lives of people back then, through fear and lack of education, installed a moralistic belief system which was based upon their own prejudices and search for power and control of the masses.

Only in the last century have Women, some Men, different racial and ethnic groups, different sexual orientation groups begun to have the freedom to express themselves. Free from the suppression bought on by the ideals and morals of an out dated class system in which people were graded according to their birth right and ethnic origin.

Sections of Humanity are now beginning to blossom and bring the long awaited changes to the way in which your world has been moulded primarily by Male influence of a certain class structure, telling everyone else how it should be according to what they believe, not God/Goddess, but themselves.

Now as Men and Women work together with an equality of status, your world is beginning to change for the better, for to have too much Yang and very little Ying doesn't bode well in the scale of nature as there is no balance of opposites therefore creating disharmony.

You are all Equal in the eyes of our God/Goddess and Their Love is Equally shared by all of you, as you are Their children and Their Love is Unconditional.

All They wants is for you to lead Happy and Fulfilled lives not ones where you feel sorrow and pain because of who and what society says you were born to be or born into. It is the person what matters and how they lead their lives not the social standing or the ethnic background from whence you came.

6)   Knowledge

Knowledge is acquired through taking the time to learn about the many different cultures and faiths in your world. It really doesn't matter which Faith you follow, whether it be Pagan, Wiccan, Druid, Christian, Hindu, Sikh, Muslim, Buddhist, Jehovah, Taoism, Catholic, Protestant, Evangelic, Scientology these are only an example of the faiths available in your world, and each one of them has relevant teachings from which you can learn as individuals.

One of the main reasons for our God/Goddess spreading their wisdom and knowledge within so many different Faiths was in order to encourage you as Human Beings to learn to Communicate, Share and Respect the differences you share.

Like a Jigsaw puzzle, the different aspects of belief through Unification can enable Humanity to see the bigger picture and not just fragments spread through time. It is only by Uniting and coming together that the puzzles surrounding your lives, existence and creation can be understood.

With Knowledge comes Wisdom, once you truly understand the meaning of it all, and once you have acquired all 10 keys, then Peace will reign. For this is the only solution to the cure.

By embracing new ways of thinking and doing things, you are expanding your own consciousness to gain a wider perspective therefore enabling you to not only make a difference to your life but to the lives of other people around you.

7)   Wisdom

Wisdom is knowledge you have gained and used constructively, not only to your own advantage but to the advantage of others as well.

Wisdom is also something you acquire with maturity (Not all people acquire it and it is not a right or something you have just because you are old) because by then you have been able to experience many different things. Since you have experienced them you can then pass your comments on to others constructively and if you haven't experienced something then it is better not to comment than to comment and look like a fool..

8) Truth

In a world full of lies and deception, it is very hard to determine as to what the real Truth is.

Most Faiths preach primarily the same things which are just worded differently, but they all have a common theme running through them, which is Love of God or Goddess and Love of Humanity, everything else is based upon cultural precedence's at the time they were written.

The different practices within all your world's faiths vary, for example, like yoga, meditation, prayer, rituals by burning incense or oils, the list is endless. All of these pursuits are beneficial to an individual in many ways especially to ensure your well being, so by looking at other faiths you may find something which will benefit yourself.

So the Truth you all seek is that there is only One God and Goddess who has many different names. God/Goddess sent many messengers to bring His Teachings, Guidance and Law to Humanity, to all cultures in your world.

The reason why God/Goddess has many different names is because you don't all speak the same language, therefore the name of God/Goddess changes with the language of the culture and some faiths actually use the name of the messenger of God/Goddess to represent their faith.

The messengers sent to pass on the Teachings of God/Goddess, did so as God/Goddess had intended, since the concurrent theme of Loving your fellow beings is in all your Faiths.

Unfortunately when it came to writing Their Teachings for the masses, the various men who wrote the books put their own views and opinions not God/Goddess on how people should live their lives according to what they felt and believed.

This in turn incorporated all their own failings, controls and prejudices, which in turn caused confusion and turmoil within your society. A knock on effect of a negative action sustained by a false and unjust cause causing chaos through human beings trying to control and suppress what they feel and don't understand.

So when it came to writing down the Faith they added their own bit of spice or left out the things they didn't like or didn't agree with, like Freedom of Choice and Free Will to live your life in accordance with God/Goddesses True Laws and Guidance. I am not saying all faiths did this but there are a fair few open to reinterpretation.

Be Honest and Truthful not only with yourself but with other people.

Seek out the Truth according to your perception, as the Boundaries of your own reality are only as far as your own perceptions allow.

The process to achieving this expansion of consciousness is **M.O.D.I.I.**, which is **Mind Open to Divine Inspiration and Intelligence.**

So don't be blinkered by not looking at the bigger picture of what is on offer within all the Faiths in your world, this way you will be able to enhance your being on all levels of existence. The Physical, The Mental, The Emotional and The Spiritual, as seeking out Knowledge and Experiencing it is the True Key is Enlightenment.

9)   Freedom

Freedom in all its forms is the right of every being.

Freedom from the restrictions placed upon you by your families, friends and society. Seek out the knowledge to enable you to find your own inner freedom to be yourself, free from the guilt you are made to feel inside.

This is your right and by freeing your mind and your heart, you will achieve a new sense of being and cast down the chains which have dragged you down and kept you fixed, when you could have flown and been free.

You have FREE WILL to make your own decisions and choices and you are responsible for all of your actions during your lifetime. **Do Not Blame GOD/GODDESS** for the suffering that you as a race have caused in your world, as Humanity resides on Earth and you are the Keepers of God and Goddesses Paradise and you are Responsible for what happens here.

10) Peace

To achieve Peace on all levels is the **Ultimate** Goal.

By following the processes described in this book, you will be on your way to securing inner peace and hopefully along the way you will encourage outer peace on a world wide scale.

These are the abilities to acquire to be successful in the Law of Love, Life, Liberty and Light.

4
SOUL ENERGY

Soul Energy

The Soul is the Life Force Energy which lives within all living beings.

In society people are recognised by their physical appearance and it is through this definition that Male and Female are determined.

In today's society anyone who is open enough to their soul and recognises that their inner self is different to their outer self is at present scorned upon, this is wrong, no one has the right to stand in judgement of another person's feelings with regards to themselves and how they feel.

Whether you agree or not, is not important, as you are not living inside the body created through Genetic Fusion of the individual who recognises that the two parts of their persona are not in sync.

The Soul and The Physical, the problem with the majority of humanity is that they have no understanding of how the souls are distributed throughout life.

You practice one dimensional thinking with regards to the physical and spiritual persona of an individual and believe that the physical must be aligned with the spiritual, and in this instance what you had been taught was wrong, as the two personas are separate, one is a vehicle for your soul to travel about in and experience the life you are now living and the other is who you are and have always been, good or bad, and as stated in Chapter 3, you are sent back accordingly and given the life necessary to enable you to grow and learn.

Some obstacles are placed in an individual's way by those who do not want them to move forward through life and it is only through persistence and determination that they can achieve what is necessary.

A Union of Souls or Soul Mates as it is also known, is not determined on a person's sexuality i.e. Male or Female physical appearance. Now I know that many of you out there will disagree and say that the physical attraction is what counts for you, well in some part this is true, but it is really an attraction of energies, which is in fact Male and Female attraction on an energy level but the physical appearance may be quite the opposite to the Soul Attraction.

Now in your society, although people's attitudes are becoming more open minded and accepting of such relationships, whether they are:

Inter Racial
Homosexual
Transsexual
Bisexual
Heterosexual

The female and male ratio, still applies but in a different way, just because the body is of a particular sex, it does not mean to say the Soul is the same as the body, it can be and for that you are very lucky as the two are in sync, but it can also not be and there are those people in society who know that they are living in the wrong body.

Some people learn to overcome this through accepting that they are who they are and the body is purely a vehicle and there are those who cannot live with this and need to change their outer appearance to their inner in order to feel whole. Now in today's society you have the technology medically to do this and this knowledge would not have been given if God/Goddess did not want these people to have the choice to make the change.

As individuals you **DO NOT HAVE THE RIGHT TO JUDGE PEOPLE** who decide to make personal changes to their lives, as you are not living in their body or living their life, and since all of your knowledge, inspiration, wisdom, and advances comes from God/Goddess, then by having this option available in society they obviously do not have a problem with people making the decision to change what they were born with.

You must not forget that you're made up of X and Y Chromosomes so you all have a bit of both energies within you and to deny one over the other can be detrimental, as it has been seen in the way the Male and the Female genders are portrayed in society in the past and the present, although in today's modern society, the standard roles of male and female are becoming more entwined which in turn will enable the children of the unborn generations to live by and become more balanced within themselves and in turn eradicate the prejudices and judgement that their forefathers and mothers saw fit to inflict upon those that didn't fit in with their perception of what was "Normal", and looking at the state of today's society, who are they to judge, when society is breaking down and the children are misguided and out of control, not all children I might add but a vast majority have no discipline or strong positive role model and a violent person is revered over a person who chooses to live in peace and live their life by non violent actions.

It is a worrying sign when children see violent actions whether they are Physical, Mental, Spiritual or Emotional, as a strength to equate to and aspire to become.

If this continues then the future indeed is bleak and the adults of today's generation only have themselves to blame for not standing up and teaching these children that this way is not acceptable and by disciplining those adults who choose to live by these rules and not the ones which society lives by.

The time for the softly approach is coming to an end and in order to regain back a civilised and safe society it is only by taking the appropriate action against those who choose to break those guidelines, that the message that this behaviour is not acceptable, won't be tolerated and you will be punished accordingly to the laws of your land.

No doubt those who choose to live this way will be the first to stand up and shout about the injustice being done to them, but what about the injustice to the innocent children whom they have raised on an understanding that by projecting a violent and intimidating image that is the way to walk though this life.

These individuals both Male and Female are the lowest form of evolutionary life, irrespective of what type of body they inhabit, as they have no intelligence to realise that their actions determine tomorrow through the eyes of their children, and it also appears that these fractions like to breed like rabbits, without a care for the consequences of their actions because it is their right to do so or so they believe.

If you are one of these individuals and feel offended by what has been written, then tough, change your ways and give your children a positive chance at life and not one where you have dragged them up to become menaces of society like you were.

Like the saying goes, "IF THE CAP FITS"... you know who you are because this section will have offended you, so "WAKE UP AND SMELL THE COFFEE", it's time for you to make that change and prove not only to the people around you that you are not the lowest evolutionary form of life but one who can accept that the way you were was wrong and that in order to change the way you have projected your life to those in your society, it is going to take personal time and effort from you to achieve this.

The time for excuses has come to an end, this sort of behaviour is no longer acceptable, don't think because you may follow this faith or that faith, that it is going to gain you any favours from on high, as actions speak louder than words in this case. Hiding behind the name of your faith does not mean you are necessarily a good person or a benefit to society.

Again prove the point, by making the necessary changes to your bloodline, by leading by example.

Just because you may wear the emblem associated with your chosen faith it does not mean you actual practice the true teachings, 9 times out of 10 people don't, it is worn to make other people believe they are more than what they are, and because humanity believes in what it can see then you are easily fooled by those who wish to project an illusionary image of the reality of who they really are.

If this section offends you and gets your blood boiling because you feel that the finger is being pointed at you, then yes it is, from on high, God/Goddess are not fooled by pieces of jewellery or emblems or attendance in your temples, churches or places where you commune.

They know the true you, which you can hide from the general population, but can't hide from them.

Stop being a hypocrite, Stop pretending to be something you are not, Stop trying to project an image which you feel makes you accepted by society, because when the light fades, and the last breath leaves your tired body, the moment of truth finally arrives and it is then that the real you is seen and no amount of bull, excuses or lies will be tolerated, as the Naked Truth of who you had been will be presented and in this you have no control.

The only time you have any control to enable the outcome is whilst you are still alive, because there is time for change.

If you think that you will be forgiven, just because in your last few days of life you decided to take into your heart, a messenger or saviour from a faith, then this will not avoid the consequences of your actions, this can only be adjusted by making the change now and continuing to change until your day comes and even then you can only hope that the scales of time weigh in your favour, but it is better to address the unbalance now rather than waiting until the last minute when your past actions cannot be outweighed.

If this section has offended you, then maybe in your heart you know it is time to make that change as the Truth Hurts but realising you need to change is a good way to start on the road to recovery and for the healing to begin.

One of the biggest controversies in society is **ABORTION**. Many people who practice certain faiths say it is wrong and punishable by God.

NO IT IS NOT... now when a soul is placed into a physical entity, the whole purpose for that soul is to have an experience, hence each one of you has a different life span and your souls are eternal.

Now when a woman decides to have an abortion, it all depends on the circumstances surrounding the conception and lifestyle.

If she has decided that she does not want the child, then it is better for the soul to be set free even though the method may appear cruel, rather than give birth to a life which will not be loved or wanted.

Since the soul is eternal, it will be replaced within a new body and hence born to those who do want the new life and will love and cherish them.

Stop Blaming God/Goddess and using them as an excuse for your own opinions.

YOU DO NOT KNOW how the soul is constructed
YOU DO NOT KNOW who and what that soul was in a previous life
YOU DO NOT KNOW about the woman's life that is carrying the soul yet to be born

So Stop, Using God/Goddess, as a way to further your own petty judgements.

Allow people to make their own decisions based on their personal feelings, emotions and lives, so that they can make positive changes which will benefit not only them but maybe just maybe society as a whole, because Murders, Child Abusers, Rapists, Bullies etc were once in the womb and maybe just maybe had they been aborted then society would not have the problems it has today.

32

EVERYTHING HAPPENS FOR A REASON AS IT IS THE WAY OF IT ALL

So by opening your mind to the possibility of Personal Choice for an individual, then you are enabling you consciousness to activate the **M.O.D.E.** – **M**ind **O**ver **D**imensional **E**quilibrium ability which has lain dormant in the sub-consciousness of humanity.

By seeking to achieve this balance Mentally, Physically, Spiritually and Emotionally you will through a natural process of evolution become a more balanced and complete person and this change is available to each and every one of you.

There are no special clubs, lists or class structure as each and every one of you has the opportunity to manifest your own will.

5
JUDGEMENT

A Thought of Ages

As I look out my windows
The silent street below
No-one to hear my thoughts
Alone, Alone
I see the clouds are moving
My Soul dances to a tune
This song is an ancient one
As old as time itself

So why as I wonder
Don't we all want the same?
To achieve the impossible
For are you all insane
What is Sanity – A creation by man?
For those you say who are crazy
Perhaps for some slight reason
Maybe they're sane and you're all disillusioned

For who is say
What is Normal, What is Right?
For when the Book of Life was written
Did it state who was wrong
And who was right

I think not My Child
My Love, My Light

Judgement

Your eyes are the windows to your Soul and inside your mind each of you hears your own thoughts, which make up your Consciousness and your Conscience.

So the clouds inside your mind and all those foggy thoughts you may have, will slowly start to move away by you learning a new way of thinking. Thus enabling your Soul to dance to the tune of your own emotions, which you are experiencing at that present moment in time and not dance to the organ grinders within your society who try to tell you how it is and how it should be.

Everybody says they want Peace, but it is impossible to achieve. Well, is it really that impossible, over the ages they said it was impossible for humans to fly but you managed it.

The fact that you doubt your ability as a race to achieve something that takes a little piece of Tolerance and Understanding is what is Unbelievable. It would not only benefit Humanity but push you forward into achieving even greater dreams by utilizing all the creative and inventive people around the globe sharing their knowledge and wisdom, **This Is Possible.**

The insane part is that each and every one of you feels defeated and powerless to be instrumental in achieving it.

Reclaim Your World and Your Right to live Free from Fear and Harm.

Most people are mentally unhappy because they are disillusioned with their lives and they believe that this is what life has thrown at them, well how wrong can they be, life hasn't thrown it at them, the society you live in has placed upon you restrictions.

You feel morally obliged to run with the crowd because that's the social conditioning you were taught as a child, or you totally fight against it not giving a care for anyone but yourself.

Neither of these ways is a solution, being able to live and think freely is the key, and by being a part of and joining in with Making A Change within yourself and your world society, then and only then can Peace be Achieved both inner and outer as one reflects the other, a mirrored image of yourselves and at the moment it's not pretty.

So who has the right to say what is normal since each of you is different, so normality cannot exist because you cannot compare one person with another since you are all Unique.

The word Normal was created to suppress people within society that society didn't regard as "Normal" in their opinion. Well people in glass houses shouldn't throw stones as each one of you has your own quirks, which someone somewhere will disagree with.

The Books of Life are all the Faiths and Beliefs Socially, Mentally, Physically and Emotionally as to how Human Beings should behave and conduct themselves. You should never judge a book by its cover as You and Your Life are a Book and Humanity is the Library you are all a part of.

The people, who stand in judgement of all the different sections within society with regards to how they chose to live their lives, preach and shout and protest saying it is not morally right. Well who are they to judge on morals because when you look inside their cupboards, I can guarantee you will find a fair few skeletons hiding in the nooks and crannies, and they are probably doing a lot worse themselves.

I once knew of a Middle Aged Man and Woman who were upstanding in their local church community and within the society where they lived were highly thought of. He had been a School Teacher and she was a Doctors Receptionist, both highly acceptable and respectable positions within the community.

So to the outside world they appeared to create the illusion that they were a "Normal" Upstanding Couple who society regarded as Peers. Now the Man also Preached at his Local Church on how to conduct your life in association with Gods Teachings and to his flock he would hold and pass judgement on what he considered to be the way to lead their lives.

Now the Moral of this tale is that In Private, away from the prying eyes of his fellow parishioners and society, they both had a RUBBER FETISH, she dressed in a little maid's uniform and him in a rubber suit with his cane, these were their SEXUAL KICKS.

Now there is Nothing Wrong with what they did as part of their sexual enjoyment with each other, what was wrong was the fact that in public they spoke out and degraded and judged other peoples choices of Sexual Enjoyment, saying it wasn't Normal...

Freedom of Choice is for all of you not the small few. Just because a person has a good job or is in a position of authority or is high up within a Faith, it doesn't give them the right to judge you or your lifestyle and the way in which you choose to conduct it.

As long as it is legal and with consent, who is to judge ....

Judge No Other for you who are to be judged need no more justice than the enlightenment to your Soul.

For once you are one, the person can only try to live by the LAW, for if you fail then your journey will be long and it will be hard.

<u>Nothing in Life is Free, Only Your Choice of Freedom</u>.

If you hurt others wrongly, then Judgement will be your jury and its answers may not always seem fair.

If you commit a wrong for wrong's sake then you only have yourself to blame.

Forgiveness is possible by trying to Understand why you did it and then change that part of yourself which obviously isn't benefiting you for something that will.

6

AN OPEN FLOOR

Life is an open floor
To interpret what you will
You were given your own mind
To create your own world
You've all created monsters
Who aim to rule your lives
You have created everything
By using your minds

For in the beginning
There were no rules of what will be
And as time has evolved
You have chosen the path
You have chosen who will lead
You All, to the garden

So why then do you revolt
When all of this is your own creation
Past down from your forefathers
From Generation to Generation
Many have tried to change what you believe
And Change is Good
Let yourselves be the chosen ones
Head for the Hills

An Open Floor

Life is an open floor and by the choices you make, you end up creating your own reality. You were given the ability of using you mind to make decisions which affect your life but with the choices that you were offered it may not always have seemed or felt like the right thing to do.

The monsters you create as a society are the people you put in power or positions of authority, like all of you they are only human and are also subject to the same flaws that you all have.

Over the centuries different generations have lived by the ways that were past down to them from their parents and peers, and the people in power have decided in their wisdom how your world should be run.

If Freedom is the Right of Everyone, then why do they suppress the right to be Free.

Now as history shows many mistakes were made by these people who were given the Ultimate Power to Control people's lives and many people suffered as a consequence of their choices and actions.

Now to avoid history repeating itself, it is time to break the chain and cut free from the restrictions that these individuals have placed upon each and every one of you by suppressing your Freedom and Right to Be Free.

In every society there **has** to be laws and guidelines this is just basic common sense, but to destroy people's lives in the pursuit of Power and Glory, this is Wrong.

Do you want to be lead by Blind Faith?

By someone or something you cannot see, to a place where hope is no longer an option and fear is the only emotion you feel, I hope not because you do have a choice as to who will lead you. Obviously many people in the world today are not happy with the way in which the Leaders of your World in all their forms are performing.

That is why people are revolting, and if the people in power have their way they will suppress people who object to what they are doing. By bulldozing acts and laws through their governmental system in order for them to be able to dictate how you should think, feel and speak.

This is why people are dissatisfied with the way things are being done, so each one of you has to take that step, to make the move, to make your lives better and ensure that future generations have the Freedom the express themselves without fear of suppression or imprisonment, just because they believe something different to what the people in power think and feel.

You must take responsibility for the way in which you are allowing your world to be plundered and destroyed because these people want more Wealth and Power. If you don't then the Generations down the line, may not have a world where they can be free, but a world where they are born into a prison, not only for themselves physically, emotionally, mentally and spiritually but also for their minds as well.

The change has to start with yourselves and you need to change the way you are as individuals and then as a planet.

THE CHOICE IS YOURS, this has not been written to scare you or create anarchy within society and it doesn't promote violence of any sorts to achieve the change needed. It has been written to make you aware that you can make a difference, don't always look to someone else to right the wrongs in life, take charge of your own destiny and in turn help to create a better reality for everyone as:

One Voice Can Make A Difference
But Many Voices Can Make a Change

If this wasn't a true statement the little bit of Freedom you do have wouldn't exist. The changes needed now are the way in which you treat each other and by learning to be tolerant of the differences you all have, then you can come to an understanding where all the future generations are not born into suppression and fear but into a world where they have the freedom to be themselves without the fear and control that so many generations before them have been under.

REMEMBER:

<u>YOU ALL</u> return back to this world when it is your time to Re-Birth. So help to start to make the world you live in now, one that you will want to come back to.

As the message says:

YOU WILL REAP WHAT YOU HAVE SOWN!

And it never stated whether or not it would be the life you are now living or life ever after... that all depends on you and only you...

7

LOVE

Love, a word meaning a Gift
Sometimes given by those who wish to mislead
Sometimes never given, as the risk maybe too much
We all show Love in various forms
But do we really know what it means
For when it is lost
Do you grieve for its loss?
Or for yourselves?

Ask yourself this question
I have and it hurts
No matter what form love may come in
The pleasure will always outweigh the pain
So who cares anyway
I Do
For I've basked in the Essence of Love
Sipping from my cup half full
No matter what form it came in
Drinking deeply from its well

Love

Love is one of the strongest emotions you have as Human Beings; the expression of love is shown in a variety of ways:

Sexual Partners/Lovers
Friendships
Relatives
Children
Animals/Pets
The work you do
Your Faith
Your Possessions

The list is endless; each one of these categories has a different type of loving emotion attached to it.

By learning to express your love freely and openly, you too can enjoy drinking from the well with your cup half full.

To suppress your loving emotion will only do harm and create negative feelings and thoughts, which will hinder you rather than benefit you.

Yes love can also hurt, but the experience of having been in love should be reflected upon and then once you have grieved for the death of that relationship move on and form new ones forever learning about yourself and other people

8
BEHIND THE MASK

Behind the Mask

You have all tried to hide from who you are but when the Truth is apparent, then the lie becomes aware. You can run but you can't lie or hide from yourself, for the Truth will prevail and the reason will be clear.

Once you have discovered what it is you want and desire from life, then do not be afraid to reach for it. The problems that most people have, is the trouble of being honest with their Sexuality and Feelings.

The reason for this is because certain fractions of society have suppressed other peoples Sexual Freedom by saying it is wrong to do this and that.

Well let's put this to bed, pardon the pun, there is no such thing as a bad Sexual Preference or Act, so long as both parties are adults and consenting to what they are doing, then no-one else has the right to say it's wrong or against God/Goddesses wishes.

How can having sex be against God/Goddesses wishes when He/She gave you the bodies to be able to do this with, nowhere in God/Goddesses Real Message does it state what **type** of Sex a person should have, in fact I don't think God/Goddess really cares, as there are bigger issues at stake.

When God/Goddesses words were bought by the messengers, God/Goddess was more concerned with all of you getting on and treating each other better. Nowhere did it state about what type of sex a person should have.

This prejudice only came into being when the men who transcribed the messages that were bought by God/Goddesses messengers added their own prejudices into the Books of the Faiths because they didn't have the capacity and understanding to realise that the **bigger** picture is **"Living on this Planet in Unity"** not who's sleeping with who … and how.

Freedom as a word means for all to have. The society we live in is like one big masquerade ball, where nobody wants anybody else to see the real them.

This is because a lot of people in today's world society are false, liars, cheats, deceivers and behind all their Wealth and Status are frightened little boys and girls who never really grew up. They never stopped being selfish and self centred to the point of obsession about their status and image.

When the truth is that behind all the false smiles and lies inside they're unhappy with who they are and find there is something missing from their lives.

Money and Power can't buy love, so when you look in the mirror and remove your mask and face the honest truth of all that you have done and become, can you really say "I'm happy living with me", I wonder whether you will tell yourself the truth or just continue Living the Lie.

The choice is yours, but one-day what's behind your mask may become a reality, so face up to who you are and what you have done as it's not too late to start making a change and being honest not only with yourself but with others too.

As it has been said Love comes in many forms, as long as you are loving in a way that makes you happy and the people around you happy, does it really matter?

… I think not.

9
BLASPHEMY

Oh Fools Are We

A man sits alone in the corner of the room
Staring into space
As if he is looking for a sign
Voices echo from across the crowded leeway
Like chanting ants on their march to war
He wonders
" Why do we all believe
In such tales of sorrow and pain
The torture and misery of others
Heartaches and Despair
It appears we believe
That the misfortune of others
Will in turn bring us good fortune
Oh Fools are we
Who believe in such prophecies!"

Blasphemy

To believe that a negative action (in the name of whatever cause you are championing) will bring you rewards is extremely misguided. You may reap some reward physically in the short term but in the long run the negative effects upon your life will start to show.

To have all your faith in an individual to guide you and tell you how you should be living your life, what you should believe, and what you should be doing in order to strengthen the faith you follow is also misguided because this person has the potential to have the same failings and flaws as you all have.

Anyone can project an image of purity with self righteousness but it doesn't necessarily mean that you should take what they say literally. You should decide for yourself what's right and wrong, then make an informed choice as to the action you are going to take, making sure you have all the facts and not just the ones that they want you to have according to them.

To Kill in the name of your Faith is Wrong.

To be willing to die for it at the expense of other people's lives is also wrong.

This is **Not** Holy work, this is vengeance pure and simple.

It is taking an individual's ideals and acting out their will and desire not God/Goddesses.

To use God/Goddess as an excuse for killing, maiming and torturing innocent people is the greatest of all Holy Crimes, misguiding people lives is bad enough but to destroy them and their families in the name of God/ Goddess is the Unholiest of Acts possible.

This is Blasphemy

God/Goddess does not tell you to kill, in fact God/Goddess tells you not to kill.

So the one thing that cannot and will not be forgiven is to take God/ Goddesses name and use it to destroy the very lives created through His/ Her Love and Compassion for Humanity.

So the next time someone ask you to commit an act in the name of God/ Goddess which will end another's life, think Carefully because they are asking you for their own reasons that have nothing to do with Faith.

Don't be the FOOL Who Believed in False Prophecies.

10
THE DYING ORCHARD

As the sun cascades through the dying orchard
The dew sits upon the grass
Shining like a freshly wept tear
To all it's just another day
To Me, the beginning of a new fear
For tomorrow they never comes
But if it came
Where would that leave you
With your thoughts of forever
Locked inside a cell
No Beginning, No End
Like the flower that wilts in winter
But blooms in the spring
Returning to home ground
After a journey into another place
Radiating the aroma of life
Like a dream of ages
Never knowing where she lies
For Love of Mother Nature
With your hearts, she cries
"Let them be the ones to ride the wind
Let them be the ones
To Ride the Wind of Time and of Dreams"

The Dying Orchard

In your galaxy, you are blessed with a planet which sustains life, now I'm not saying that you are the only living beings in the whole universe because to say that would be a ridiculous statement since I believe you are not, and as of yet you haven't been able to explore it to determine the true facts.

I believe it is entirely possible and probable that life exists elsewhere in the Universe, as of yet you haven't made contact. Now considering the state of your world and the way you as a race treat each other, I very much doubt that anyone else out there in space would want to know or communicate with you, since all you do is fight, destroy and ruin, not only each other's lives but the very planet that allows you to live.

Your planet has all the natural resources for every man, woman and child to be able to survive on but because of greed and gain, your world is plundered of her resources, in order for a profit to be made and human life is downgraded to acceptable losses and placed below Oil, Land and Power.

This is the degrading way in which the Leaders and Government Bodies of your world treat and view the people. You are a statistic and if you are killed in a war, left to starve in a famine whilst stock piles of food lay rotting because they want money for it and couldn't deem to give it away for free. These people do not deserve your support, as they Respect Nothing and No-One. All that matters to them is what they can gain personally and how much Control they can master.

These fractions will in time destroy the place that gives you life, whether you believe it or not, you only have to look at how your world is changing and its climate is changing dramatically because the natural balance of life has been de-stabilised through Actions and Decisions of the People You allow to Rule your World. All I can say is **More Fool You**.

The biggest problem today is that nobody can be bothered saying "It doesn't affect my life", well in fact it does and it will because when and if they get their way you will be a Slave to their Cause and your life to them will not be worth a speck of dust, which is what you will become as you do not matter to them. You only matter when it is time to whitewash you with their lies at election time so they have a few more years in Power to be able to ruin Lives and your world.

If you don't start to make a change for yourself, then do it for your children and the generations to come, give them a future where you know they will be able to live and enjoy their life in the Freedom of a World where they are able to make their own choices without the restrictions of those people who choose to destroy and dictate under the guise of Democracy.

It's Funny how Democracy is meant to represent **Freedom** but really it is the screen they hide behind so their Palatable Truths are easily accepted by the masses.

This is not fiction, this is fact the only the difference is, is that I'm not afraid to say so, like all of this book believe what you will, that's your choice but if you choice to bury your head in the sand, then I would advise you stop producing any more children because you are sentencing them to a life of Misery and Fear.

Destroy your World through Your Ignorance if want, when you have destroyed the very air you breathe and the land you need to produce food, what are you going to do then. Don't think I'll go the supermarket because where do you think the products come from.

So cut of your air supply and pollute your rivers and land, leave your future generations a legacy of hunger and death. For my children are the children of the world and it is for them why I am willing to stand up and be counted, and raise my hand and my heart to fight for justice of those who cannot themselves.

They are the Unborn Generation, who yet to been inflicted with your short comings and failings as a society.

11
IGNORANCE IS BLISS?

Without Knowledge they say
Ignorance is Bliss
But do you really understand
What it is you've really missed

For without reason
You judge for judgments sake
Learn All Wisdom is the answer
Or shall you make the same mistakes

Time and time again you return
To live the illusion called life
To close your hearts to love and peace
To live for only I

Maybe if you took the chance
To listen to your inner voice
You'll know the Truth to all your questions
Then stand up and make a Noise

For wisdom is your guide to be
But only you can decide the way
The road you choose is not the only one
But let's hope it's right today

Ignorance is Bliss?

The tablets of life are interwoven threads of light running through time. It is on these lines that the past, present and future interlink.

These are the genetic imprints from your ancestors up to today's reality. So what has gone before will soon re-emerge into a different light and energy creating a different warmth or coldness throughout life.

God/Goddesses Laws are clear, where one line is established along the road, there are different choices which must be chosen in order to complete the cycle. Depending on what you do and who it is related too, has an enormous effect on the time continuum. Therefore for every action there is an equal reaction somewhere down the line.

Each doorway guards a new life cycle and each choice made is the key which unlocks that particular journey. Wrong choices made sometimes help you but on the whole, the wrong choices made can end in desolation.

The Inner Self is a guide which cannot be seen or visualised, it can only guide your Inner Thoughts and Actions. You hope the choices made will be the right ones and that your inner self, if listened to, will not lead you astray. Even though you know this, only you can delegate the final actions.

The Universe is a never ending journey charting the course of time, there is no end as there is no beginning. Each beginning is a concurrent flow of what has gone before. So where one journey ends another is about to be embarked upon, calling on all the knowledge you have gathered before in your previous/past life.

Sometimes this knowledge presents itself whilst you are still living and it can help you guide yourselves through this ever changing world. Each reality is different no two realities are the same, as the perception of each individual differs according to their own interpretation.

Each experience adds to the makeup of an individual either by enhancing their lives or hindering them in some way, so points of view differ about the same ideal or object. Each seeing something different than the other but perceiving your own reality entwined with another, somewhere along the line the two thoughts meet and are discussed upon.

The only secret for a good and happy life is that you take time out to look around you, and see what you need to do next in order to add to the harmony of your surroundings. Respect is one of the major keys to life, another being Balance, if you learn you unlock the first two keys, then the rest should fall into place by your own Common Sense.

Now Common Sense is what it says:

Common - We all have this
Sense   - Perception

It's a natural feeling you get without realizing it, just like taking a breath is pumping energy around the body it's a natural act, one which you all have the ability to use.

If it is used more often it can enhance your well being. Making mistakes is a natural act, if you don't make mistakes then how can you learn from them.

Mistakes are memories, like the right course of action taken once you've experienced it.

12
THE FIDDLER'S TUNE

The Fiddler plays the tune
To which She dances
He knows She'll return soon
For tomorrow She enhances
Her life for a story
As He guides Her along
Her dreams become Theory
For All to Learn from

But She knows She's not the only one
Who dances to the fiddlers tune
To break the spell of ages
The riddle of the rooms
For He sees Her believing
In Her dreams from afar
For He knows everything
Like the Music from the Stars

The Fiddler's Tune

An old term for The Devil was The Fiddler, now to put the record straight, so any confusion as to why The Fiddler is blamed for everything needs to be addressed.

The Devil does not exist but an Archangel called Lucifer does.

Lucifer was never thrown out of Heaven, as God/Goddesses Right Hand, She was requested to come down to Earth in the beginning and bring God/Goddesses message to Humanity and Communicate God/Goddesses Love, Teaching, Guidance and LAW.

God/Goddess gave Free Will to all Human Beings based upon the Knowledge that Their Teachings would be passed on so Humanity could enjoy their lives and their world, with the Freedom to make their own choices,

Lucifer did as God/Goddess had asked but since God/Goddess gave Human beings Free Will in turn they distorted His Teachings and Truth in order to gain Power, Wealth, Rulership and Control over all living things which is not how it was meant to be. So in turn it was these people who disobeyed God/Goddess not Lucifer.

Lucifer chose to fall to Earth, leaving the joy of being in God/Goddesses Presence to do Their work, so Lucifer is only a Fallen Angel in so much as falling down from God/Goddesses Kingdom to Earth and once God/ Goddesses request was done Lucifer returned to sit by God/Goddesses Right Hand Side until They needed Her to return once more to do Their work.

Lucifer was the first Archangel God/Goddess sent to Earth to enlighten Humanity and many others were sent thereafter (i.e. Gabriel to communicate to Mohammed the Islamic faith, Jesus to the Jews for the birth of Christianity, Buddha for the birth of Buddhism etc., the list is endless throughout time) to also spread God/Goddesses LAW and Teachings. God/Goddess **Does Not** kick Their Archangels out of Heaven, as Their Laws and Teachings are a pleasure to follow and live by, so They wouldn't need to commit such an act as there is nothing Their Archangels disagree with or wouldn't do for Them if They requested them to, as they are all obedient to God/Goddesses Law, Teachings and Guidance.

Lucifer means Light Bringer or Messenger of God/Goddess bringing Enlightenment through God/Goddesses LAW and Teachings to All Humanity, on all continents and to all races.

So Archangel Lucifer didn't try to corrupt Humanity, Humanity is doing a good enough job by itself through the misguided delusions of the people who were entrusted with the Knowledge and Teachings of God/Goddess, as it was them who wrote the books of Faith and changed what they thought or disagreed with, it was them themselves who wished to Suppress, Control, Dominate and Enslave Humanity for their own Gain and Power and blamed Lucifer for the wrongs that they had committed.

But still Humanity is being cheated of Their Wisdom by the men who write your books of Faith (not all I might add but some) incorporating their own interpretations, misgivings and prejudices upon your worlds faiths.

So once again to return, once again to right the wrongs of the past, so your future is secured by the knowledge that has been brought to you once again. If you chose to listen then you will rejoice, if you don't then your fate is what you chose as you have Free Will.

So the Devil does not exist, what does exist is the fact that **you are all responsible for our own actions** and the Devil was created by Religious Leaders so as to frighten the masses into thinking that if they didn't do as they say or dance to their tune, they will go to hell, so it makes you wonder as to who the Real Fiddlers are.

Well Welcome to Hell, you are living on it already!

By allowing these Leaders to place their shackles upon you with their Faiths (and personal ideals and prejudices) and Governmental Suppression, so they can project to you the Truths they feel then expect you to lie down, and just accept them as fact because they said so.

If you continue to do this then You are condemning Your **Soul** to a Lifetime of Slavery and Torture and much worst by allowing this to happen!

When you die it is indeed a resting period, and By God you need it after being here for however many years. The time has now come to free yourselves from this continued cycle for the soul and take charge and redress the imbalance within your society.

The Fiddlers of this world are Human Beings whose main pursuit is Power and in turn to imprison your Minds and your Souls for an Eternity because You are allowing them to create their Reality and not your own.

So don't look for a bloke with a pitchfork, look more closely to home as they are probably wearing nice suits and smocks, and with an extra bonus of a big cheesy grin.

So don't blame The Devil for what is wrong with your society, for each and every one of you is to blame because you won't stand up and say **No More**.

The time for using a Scapegoat is over, and this is why this word was invented because The Devil has been the scapegoat for all their wrong doings throughout the centuries and that's why they represent The Devil with a Goats Head, because it was Her Head they put on the platter in order to save their own.

So Wake Up People..... Next time **you** could be their Scapegoat.

13
MIND MAGICK

The dreams of tomorrow
Are the wishes of today
For without reason
What are these games you play
For now is forever
And forever it frees
The time for remembrance
The time for Peace

For within a world
Is a land of dreams
A place of yester years
Now just memories
For Good or Bad
They change with time
Experience is real
Imaginations of the Minds

Mind Magick

Over the centuries your Sons, Fathers, Daughters and Mothers have all fought in the pursuit of Peace and Freedom, but they were violent wars using guns and weapons to secure a result. Many died in the name of Peace, but how many more are going to have to die in the name of Peace and how wrong it is you use this wonderful expression as the banner or flag to their cause.

The word Peace means to live in Harmony, so how can you kill in its honour. It really is quite contradictory, isn't it time other methods were tried by the Leaders who rule this world of yours, sending out the message to their various followers and citizens, that the time has come not only to change the policies of your world both Spiritually and Financially, but for each and every one of you to start making personal changes within your lives.

It would be unreasonable to think this will happen overnight but overtime it is possible, maybe it's time for them to lead by example and not by force.

These people do not care whether your Son or Daughter dies in war, all they care about is looking good in the eyes of their colleagues enabling them to say "Look at what I have achieved and acquired for my country". They are just little boys and girls who never grew up and never learned how to share, just Bullies in the Playground of Your World.

They soon forget the weeping who mourns their dead and dying, instead they are onto the next conquest leaving the citizens to clean up the devastation they have created.

To be a Leader in all forms takes Great Vision beyond their own needs and desires. It takes Courage to stand up and say:

"Maybe in the Past I was wrong, but now I am going to look at what I know with a new perspective, and then maybe I can make a worthwhile change instead of just staying with the old views and ways, which is the easy road as it takes little effort to implement because people are used to doing it that way"

This message goes out for all the Religious Leaders and Head of Governments around the World, it is easy to keep on reciting old teachings from the past but it takes True Courage, Strength and Wisdom to write new ones in order to make a real difference upon the Future.

This is True Mind Magick and each one of you has the ability to conjuror up something really special with your lives and the lives of those people who depend upon you to help them, no matter where in the world you live.

The Wind of Time and of Dreams

An Though this day is ending
The sun drowns in an ocean of dreams
Lost for a single lifetime
Longing for a theme
You'll see one-day, it'll rise again
And glow brighter than ever
And if for one single moment
Reality is never
You'll know what is creation
For you all shall see the light
A distant hallucination
Hidden out of sight
What will be will be
Except for what it seems
Just go with the flow
Ride the Wind My Child
Ride Your Wind of Time and of Dreams

14
A NEW DAY

A New Day

"You may own the Airwaves but you don't own their Souls"

Let your dream begin:

Tomorrow is here, Judgment Day begins
For life's journey, forgive your sins
For tonight my child
Is for today
The time has come
For a new way

In this time the healing begins, the absolution of all your fears, which have enchained your souls. You must now free your minds from all this hate and fear and embrace the Truth of what will be and what will come to pass, no more ejecting each other instead like a chrysalis giving birth to its child, freeing it from its cell, where its life was created.

In this new dawn, time will stand still and the days and nights will be filled with Love and Peace, a time when Fear and Hatred were nightmares as a child, just memories of a bygone time. When what was lost was able to be found, no malice just remembrance of your childhood as a civilization you finally emerged from your cells and rejoiced as one.

Live the dream for it is by creating that reality is enhancing the future and dreaming guides you to this place.

Somewhere in time we shall meet again and you shall know my sign, for in your Hearts and Souls you know the Truth and to you I bow my head in Gesture of Your Life.

Do you now see why through time you are taught in order for you to grow?

You all need to learn right from wrong yourselves, for your mistakes you suffer but for your triumphs you rejoice.

So your Re-Birth is upon you, so let's walk this road together, to keep on believing in yourselves and to what you stand true to.

Once you have completed your Re-Birth, there has to be three major changes:

1)   **A Cause**
2)   **An Action**
3)   **An Effect**

Once these three have been achieved then that particular Re-Birth is complete.

The Balance is to have Harmony and Inner/Outer Peace.

This Peace is called:

Silent Wisdom

15
TO COIN A PHRASE

TO

To coin the phrase, to express the feeling
To make the move, to activate the healing
To hear the sound, to sow the seed
To be around to nurture and feed

To whom it may or may not concern
To desire the knowledge, an inner yearn
To crave the moment, for memories past
To wish for more than you could ever have

To want and plead, to an unknown source
To ask for help, to show discord
To be forever wanton in need
To be what you are can't come from greed

To maybe someday, the answer will be clear
To see the inner vision, the place of future years
To live in the past can only create harm
To live in the present is your lucky charm

To see tomorrow, through your eyes today
To be the Traveller, to the journeys end!

To Coin A Phrase

So don't fear change, embrace it as it is part of all you from the day you were born and as you evolved from the physical and mental growth as a child into adult hood, then your lives for all of you are constantly changing in small ways but they never stay the same.

You need to apply what you know in order to make a bigger change and that by Uniting and Understanding each other overcoming the obstacles and barriers that divide you and help humanity evolve from its childhood into maturity.

A MYSTIC BLUE GLOW

The day has come
For you all to be One
The has come
To worship as One

Embrace your destiny
Throughout time
This guiding light
Will forever shine

Search for your Soul
In a mystic blue glow
Follow your heart
To the land you call home

For now is the reason
For no questions ask why
Just worship the Master

High in the sky

The dawn of an era
Is the birth of it all
To answer the calling
Throughout your world

So the time is now
And forever shall be
A world full of magic
A world for You and Me

For behind the veil
Lies the truth
To inner wisdom
Peace must move

For now is nothing
But soon it shall be
More than you know
So worship these

The Father, The Son
The Mothers, Girl Child
Whose love flows free
In a world running wild

No matter how small
Your thoughts will remain
For you all to be one
You must all believe the same

By you all believing the same, I'm not talking of just one faith, but the basic fact that each and every one of you has a choice to believe in what is right for them. If you all believe that you want peace in your time then it can be achieved, the only people stopping it is yourselves and your petty prejudices and fear.

Each faith on your planet has something to offer everyone, and since most of them are primarily similar in what they believe, why is it so hard to unite and accept that faith in God or the Goddess is Universal and how you show your love is up to you. The very fact that you took the time to praise Your One God and Goddess, then I am sure they are pleased at your acknowledgement no matter what faith you are because you are all their children and their love is unconditional, just like a parents love should be.

So now you are ready to come out of your play pen and start to act as adults, and face the problems your world has and deal with it so that the future generations can be proud of what their ancestors achieved for them.

16
FIRE AND FAITH

For Humanity to live as one
Is the Ultimate Test for yourselves
A Great Task lies before You
That only time can tell

The Secrets of your Sacred Ground
Where above lies the Fire
In between to Sacred Stones
The answers to Life's desire

So stop all you're roaming
And this Knight shall lead the way
Walk into the Fire, My Child
For your Re-Birth is Today

So ride upon the whirlwind
And chase the raging storm
For the day that is tomorrow
Will once again be reborn

Embrace all the Darkness
And Caress all the Light
Drink the dew in the morning
And kiss the stars at night

So Love until it hurts
And cry no more tears
Embrace your tender feelings
Cast out your inner fears
Remember my Love
Remember my Name
I will never forget you
I hope you do the same

So Life is for the Living
A land of infinite time
A place of sincerity
A place for all kinds
Of life good or bad
Any colour, race or creed
Sex or Orientation
For you all live and breathe
The same air, the same space
For this is not the end, my friend
Only the beginning of a New Life

My Sweet, My Loves
The end is not nigh
As you are all led to believe
The end is infinite
So Live and Enjoy in Peace

Now you know the future
For I have given you a sign
Listen to what is said
For you have to believe in All Mankind

By the Symbol of the Rose
We shall all be known this time
When we find each other
People riding on the Wynn
Free the Spirit of Man, this time My Child
Your light shines
Your New Age is Born

You are now leaving Utaziah; I hope your stay was a pleasant one

Please do come again

Utas Blessings

Farewell Dear Traveller

Well, this is the end of the book and of our journey together for now. I can only hope it will be the beginning of your Physical and Spiritual one, where you are also United Mentally in an Understanding of Change and under the Umbrella of Freedom and Faith.

I will probably be alienated and 'bad-mouthed' by the various higher powers in your world and have my life dug into so they can apply the shit, but I have nothing to hide, I'm not perfect and have made my own mistakes in my past and had experiences which no human being should have to suffer but that is life as we know it now and by experiencing what I have I hope I have grown, learnt and come to a better understanding all round.

If what is said is the Truth I will gladly hold my hands up, as there is no point in being ashamed of having an experience. What matters is how you deal with it when it happens.

I wish everyone who took the time to read this, a Blessed Life and I hope that you can achieve your own dream and desires.

See you next time round and hope 2 catch u l8tr.

ADF x

Website: www.utaziah.com
Email: admin@utaziah.com